OM KRISHNA II

OM KRISHNA II

OM KRISHNA II

from the
Sickroom
of the
Walking Eagles

CHARLES HENRI FORD

CHERRY VALLEY EDITIONS

This book was made possible, in part, by funds from the New York State Council on the Arts.

Produced at Open Studio (187 East Market Street, Rhinebeck, N.Y. 12572), a non-profit facility for writers, artists and independent literary publishers, supported in part by grants from the New York State Council on the Arts and the National Endowment for the Arts.

Library of Congress Cataloging in Publication Data

Ford, Charles Henri.
    Om Krishna II: From the Sickroom of the Walking Eagles.

    I. Title.
PS3511.0392044   811'.52   80-13972
ISBN 0-916156-48-6 sp. sgd. hdbk.
ISBN 0-916156-47-8 pbk.

Cherry Valley Editions may be ordered directly from The Book Bus, Visual Studies Workshop, 31 Prince St., Rochester, N.Y. 14216.

Sections of this book were first
published in Sun & Moon,
Pearl, Rejection and Gay Sunshine.

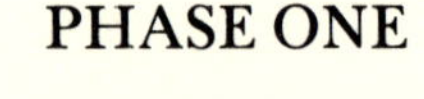

PHASE ONE

THE ILLNESS

I

The thousand-hooded one sleeps quietly his big toe
     in his mouth
There is nothing godlike about him except the lines
    of his body
A sword is by his side a bloody scarf has been thrown
    away
Flower wristlets and crown of falcon feathers are
    unruffled
Once you have breathed in the scent of his clean-
    shaven cranium
You realize that what has to be done had best be done
    quickly
Finding yourself in a world in which there are only
    two people
You have traded the karma which comes from non-
    possession
To be but the bone of each other's bone
After breaking the pot of butter and giving it to the
    monkeys
A child flies out the window
He will set a noose round the fangs
Of the Guardian of Cosmic Law
Family secrets exist no longer than quills on a toad

II

With the drug of sleep to lock you in the dream
A special loss returns to the one who never went
    away
New born monster with gruesome grin
And teeth that severed his own umbilical cord
Surprised in the presence of former torturers
In a voice of georgette crêpe he asks

May I borrow your dry-disc rectifier
He had the thrill of standing behind the images
A deployment of mystification
If you're not goodlooking something went wrong
I don't know what you're talking about
He continues to turn the unnumbered pages
Glancing up with watery eyes that miss nothing
Whenever an aggressive onlooker growls

III

He was not born he was dragged out
Perfectly formed and colored like a sky-blue lotus
Fed with a lump of cotton soaked in honey
It was the eighth day of the somber half of the month
Cows painted green with gold and silver leaves on
       their horns
Grazed near the river Alanada which sings at night
A young anchorite immersed in the Quest of the
       Supreme
Lead the caparisoned horse to Kalinga
A goat made of straw stands amidst burning candles
Majestic hump rising like the lingam of Mahadeva
I will ride him said Krishna
Over Hotel New Picnic a halo of miraculous power
The game becomes a work of art there are counter-
       strategies of mud and poinsettas
Doors are opened by unseen hands

IV

In the first stage of initiation the inserted-tooth cutter
Consolidates the flash butt welding
An embossing hammer starts with clamp coupling

Magnetism of inverted spin with high gloss gauge
Krishna keeps watch on reptiles for signs of disaster
A feather dances in his diadem
Polysubstitution may also appear
Between the folds of gang tools used on planes and
        latches
Rope stretchers of translucent overthrust
Modules of rigidity at high temperature
Pressure stops for slit fricatives
And plaster casts compounded with gum water
Plexiform cloacas are still in ferment
The prime condition for a left-hand screw

V

Civilized decency has no middle leg
Signs and portents come in plain wrappers
Beginning with toads and climaxing with sadhana
Followed by fish-stick liquor from foreign seeds
Volume changes in the lungs of a hybrid hen
Involve several purification steps
On a two-roll mill polar wandering provides less
        payload
Like seeing the logic of the illogical — illogically
In preparing the waste for disposal
Crossover probabilities are paramount
Whether inspiration occurs on the top or down stroke
In males there is more abdominal involvement
Manipulation of the primary beat
Do you love me your respiratory pigments say yes

VI

Entranced by the prospect of Gonidia
The Jerusalem rag-head worked at his basketry
A broken sleeve held his right arm back
With the left he starts popping his cakes
Dismissing all thought of improved livestock
The phosphates of freedom
In accents of alternate moan and bellow
Leave their neurograms on the palisade
A sex mosaic in time a mock-poetic menotaxis
The inner veil lifted on pectoral perfection
Exterior undulation revealing
Egg-envelopes before they become shells
The reason for the incidence has not been determined
Another turn in the life history of an overlapping
    irritant

VII

Mother Saraswati is pounding the pavement of Heat
    Street
Going to gather ash-blue beach plums (Krishna has
    two of his own same size shape and color)
On the Dunes of the Ocean of Learning (her true
    domain)
Those bearded crows of nostalgia won't go away
But she is not disturbed by their cawing
They cannot fly so high as Garuda of the golden
    wings
He must be a deity to have a head like a bullet
To some he is fearful as the I Ching were it infallible
To others he is a disrobed king wearing Balarma
    briefs

Two apprentice ascetics join the caravan to Karavirapura
Eagle faces and sacriligious hankerings
Whatever they hope will happen must be met half
    way
Cast in heroic mold they are able to stand steady in
    a moving chariot
Rubber bands on their index fingers help work
    wonders

VIII

In an acid bath mingled with mollusca
Bulbous extremities call for hog-back riding
Expert accomplishment of the practised vagrant
Slated for an ice-drift in juvenile waters
The long-range planner of a second Aghia Sophia
Gazing upon the ground with wave-out musings
Wears the warning wardrobe
Found in American comics (incredible foulness)
Cinnabar boots and pull-apart spurs
Ejactmenta from some personal hydrosphere
Shining with desert dust
Parachuting around us
Containing his catch of whiptail flounder
With a polyphonic keypunch sifter of Magma &
    Jade

IX

A cowherd's hand can be magical
Five digits seductive as undetected talent
Flaring effectively a budding romance
Fingernails less obliterated than the claw of a toe

Index knuckles unassertively devoid
Of hardline insouciance
The noises of nature which accompany liaisons
Of muscle and bone
Like any alternative pathology
Oblivious to vestiges of whale-blubber grace
Bravery functions when unsolicited
A situation commonplace as malnutrition
Aggression depending upon the coercion
The more successful when no word is heard

X

(for James Merrill)

A war for Dharma is waged with flower-tipped arrows
Gopala the Cerulean
Like a sheep fragrant with sandal paste
Represents vows of asceticism
He resembles Kamadeva the God of Love
Clothed in a tasselled tunic
Shakra a small groom lanky but sturdy is being led
        to the altar
On his forehead the mark of sanctified ashes
Shishupala who hates the smell of horses is waiting
        there
Murderously impatient like the copper cutlass which
        he holds in one hand
Only the arrival of the Princess of Karavirapura
Having closed her eyes to the ruin of her own life
Transforms what was meant to be a memorial to the
        disc of the rising sun
Into a puja for the wax-winged Icarus I am sorry but
        your banana leaf has been flooded

XI

He sits working at finding the root of the ideal
     number
There's nothing this boy can't do
And little that he won't attempt
His alternate segment a constant dilation
Bone inductions were felt in his chest pulse
At the center of similitude his ground speed is near
     the limit of integration
In the circle of closest contact
His is the parabola of safety
With an outwash fan creating a nuée ardente
He preserves the animal cry theory
At the cluster point no kink-band keeps his succus
     entericus in check
He wrote the letter in immigrant dialect using Arabic
     script
Towards eleven o'clock I left a message for him to
     meet me at the Lab of Spherical Excess
It is 12:45 I don't know if he called back while I was
     out

XII

Bashful little beast you've taken the top off the bread
If this is his initial plunge into suburbia send him
     back to the bayou
Codicles and guavas are waiting in welcome
Instead of gaping at blast-hole drills and earth-
     moving equipment
Or eating too much of something he knows is bad for
     him
He can play all day with disabled ex-servicemen
As great an object lesson as the dynamics of a locust
     invasion

The presence of chicken-pox may be defined with a
        dip stick
After searching for the life jacket under his seat
Krishna Bahadur was first to enter the box containing
One million signatures in favor of the death penalty
You are fantastic Angel Cordero tells him
He moves from the tiger claw shilva to the double
        wrist block
Before descending the pneumatic staircase leading
        to corporal punishment
A rationalization of possibilities below the backbone

XIII

At the Misty Sauna Baths he was angry because he
        went unrecognized
Taking his coat off he sat under a table and refused
        to budge
Until the surgeon observed if the road is dangerous
        you may not come back
But remember I have left it to your honor
The teacher divided the pomegranate between the
        two of them
It was a disillusioning experience to find that the one
        on whom he had lavished gifts
Responded neither with affection nor gratitude
Menage amidst primitive surroundings
Gilded trappings and soiled fustanellas
After draining his snake he drove the turkeys to
        market
And returned with a ping-wing device purchased at
        the Lucky Emporium
Will this pale brute ever come round to being re-
        spected

He said to himself I shall sit by the temple in front
        of my house
And swallow in one capsule a dehydrated five-course
        dinner

XIV

The raids were shared with Kamiwazumi
Through the bunghole of a breeding cage
Sunakhari's shaft did a lot of dry grinding
Having thrown a number of quads with the nick up
Instead of waiting to drive the ball inside the D area
Dambar Chandra's cover-point went limp
The nailhead spar didn't register
Signs of a dorso-uvular operation were spotted and
        thwarted
Shiva's arithmetico progression was savaged
The dovetail position proved effective for a while
Heteromorphous and inducing permeability
There are no sounds of any kind in space
A question of constitutional variables
Krishna is the air itself without him music would not
        be possible

XV

Distractions in the forest
Developed a sense of exhaltation
Cord muscles slithered towards the sun
Scents of other glands subtleties of pleasure and pain
It is inauspicious to shed tears when saying goodbye
In the wake of those from whose feet the dust is
        wiped and laid on our eyes

To be depressed by nothing is to go to bed with
       everything
Including pendulous hydrocysts
Interspersed with swollen bodies from the sacral hollow
Nerves at the fingertips are the last to be blunted
Old as the most uncontrollable of the elephants
One who knows the intimacy of right and wrong
Shares with him blood siphoned from sleeping
       rabbits
His lotus eyes live only for the moment

XVI

Ghana Shyam cast the horoscope of the Dark One
Knowing that whoever is unaided by Dharma must
       die
Through some turn of fate stemming from neither
       player
He folds his turban and fixes it at a tilt then a
       peacock's feather must be found
I have also to make faces at boys of my own age when
       they come to accost me
Harichandra accepting new experience as if accus-
       tomed to it all his life
Wants nothing for himself that is why he is powerful
The great love he receives
He shares with those around him
You who dote on children command their affection
The interstate cheat will not be invited to the feast
       of sequestered butter
Dishonorable conduct on the football field and silver
       prices spurt
Simulacra of candles the only source of light
The boy who kicks over the cart will have been fed
       with rice and ghee

XVII

One reason for nature's attraction and repulsion
Apochrypha of anyone's lifeblood
Is the glandular tunica intima
Govinda is much taken with the animal world
He romps for hours on the savannah
Whatever podosoma he runs across
He brushes with his pollen brush
Fascination with external sacs
More pronounced in the male
Leads him into protomorphic folly
The marvelous thing about the chroma-clear raster
Anyone may benefit from its macrobiotic qualities
If you wish to solve the riddle of his charm
It's not what he does it's what he lets you do

XVIII

An everyday consideration of the Siamese twins
During foetal life they migrate
The lineality of excitement is never a single event
To test the endurance of duplicated occurrences
Routine beating comes later
Each is anti-self to the other
Knobs with a repulsion-induction motor
Two coils in the same resistance box
Suspended though not free
Inhale-exhale from the battery of molded products
Flux batches of duality
Created to eat the world leaf by leaf
Nourishing the mechanics of structureless strain
The atrocity of castration reserved for them alone

XIX

Where is Govinda tell him to come here
Krishna is first in his class he wears a Nepali cap
Nowadays everyone is in favor of female education
They're all dripping for it have a cramp in the rick
But keep your cunt hooks off my belongings said the
        pile-driver
The gold of this pendant is pure
I saw three bunches of grapes
As free of sense as one of the Führer's boys
        galloping his antelope
Down on the esplanade something will be stirring
With that extra two inches after you're forty
Though you may not be fit to carry guts to a bear
You're not donkey-rigged for nothing
A peacock dances in the wildwood
While two studs hurt each other taking it in turn

XX

Growing up was more rectogenital than anything
        else
In this respect I was as normal as the other pushrods
Pompetta my childhood sweetheart never got over
        not having married me
Still very close even ultra-basic
We enjoy horrifying imagery for its own sake
Just as we did in the jing-jang stage
One of our metasomatic experiences
Was to hold open seed vessels
Indeoglandular development being germinal
If the check nut were loosened this could go on
        indefinitely

The prolabium of the one disintegrating into the
        multipolarity of the other
While she grew polyandrous
I craved no mucus-lined progeny
With my retrocerebrality I was my own offspring

XXI

Invited to sample the charms of the vagrant harem
        Krishna has a beat on
Palazzo Morenigo is not that much different from
        Bird's Foot Delta
Quarrelling servants drenched with mango flowers
Sorting out heavy goods abandoned under the equator
The fog-bow over the dew pond is a gravity anomaly
From the composite landscape back-scuttle encroach-
        ment
A micromutation of the slip-off slope
Presumably sensuous and glaucous
Baffling blood-stained angels in their effort to scrub
        the scud
With soft hail couched in clear ice
Shout to the Spectre in Rebel Gray
If the sky falls we will catch the larks
But he went wandering in the buried forest
Running the risk of being mistaken for ductile clay

XXII

The ashes of age having disappeared
Massage the bulbo-inferences!
Transitions grow in chains
Out of Old Calcutta we rode the Juggernaut Express
Creating a sense of catastrophe

Penetralia of throes and throbs
The hospital bus was the one we took to the Sun
          Temple at Konarak
Dressed in tight-strung thongs like the god of Love
Palms salivated with gems of the infralabia
Krishna cool as a bleached bone in the moonlight
Knows how to enter the hearts of animals
Follows the sound of footsteps through mansions and
          marketplaces
She went to the parapet and closed her eyes
He bit his lips till the blood came then walked away

XXIII

His Satanic Majesty is ignorant as hell
Curious about Krishna he summons him to the zona
          radiata
Strobile as a ghost at gravity transport the conversation
Is recorded on the typewriter by the King's secretary
          Miss Hyena
(A xerox of the transcription is in the Homogenetic
          Archive at the Humanities Center)
Royal words are not wasted the leading questions
          were three
Krishna's answers endless as the ribbon of the
          universe
The first inquiry spoken in spiny-rayed vocables
          was this
What is your native element
The second what is the length of your root
The third what would be your choice between a
          captured river
And a tigroid ornament of swarm spores

With suprapubic aplomb the puer of testicular
    exploits
Enunciated his ripostes
Calculations for fire-cracked ears

XXIV

(for Indra Bahadur)

Not only a miracle of beauty but a worker of miracles
Chief performer in the fate of all his loves
Glorious inexhaustible fascinating
A monarch of the serpent race with headdress of
        brass
Like divine Poetry (the Indra of Literature)
You've got it or you get it no one can give it to you
It's the mastery of the Eagle
A toy of black marble under a heap of flowers
Soma the moon takes a ceremonial bath
The flute which hypnotized the High Priest of the
        Demons is silent
In another part of the palace the daughter of my
        uncle finds fault with the seafood
The widow of his stepbrother stands on the
        kettledrum enacting samsara
To stage a massacre in anger is madness
Why did Bedi insist on battling at number eleven in
        the Queen's Park Oval Test match

XXV

He taunts he disrupts he wins
Held in readiness was a Knight Sacrifice
And sausages to unlock the mystére
The skin of the moonlander is beginning to peel
Routine procedures of dissection are respected

Squatting in a house in Paddington human gorilla
    crossbreeds are without volition
And they have no tails
Alexander in India needed a jugular incision
Shing Moo drank himself into a stupor
Careless of the urgency of prepared variations
Lamps produce a vibrational pallor
With pustules of injecta to lay a speckled egg
More effective than any listening device
In an ambuscade of writing in the wings

XXVI

(for Ira)

The roaming masseur wears a peaked hat
After a sensuous massage of unknown potential
Devaki's offspring only smiled
His beach chair with a locked drawer for valuables
    had been stolen
When you do not know what to do that is the moment
    to accomplish very much
In reverential prostration he fell at the feet of the
    Presence
Who with a gesture of infantile tenderness
Reminded him that life is meant to be lived
The Horse Sacrifice is something to be taken seriously
Fiery as the finish of a little black hole
Subtle as salt
Or the chimes of withered leaves
Alabama trimmed Georgia one to nothing
There will always be no known survivors

XXVII

No one staggers with impunity over the rocks of the
  foreland
Except for Om Krishna who can leave his footprints
  in forest marble
And whose amethyst faeces go uncensored
Prized as gastroliths from another world
Tonight we sleep on the storm beach
True thickness will be sorted from the false
Volcanic necks support superimposed folding
Even from a half-clad adolescent lapping a zabaglione
You have promised yourself never to become an
  habitual
Offender like your elder brother Vishnu with whom
  you seem to be at cross-purposes
He's the one who dwells kinematically apart and is
  therefore taken for a star
While you pass your time adoring the unanswerable
As the giant girlchildren do
Watching the strolling boys walking so slow not
  going anywhere

PHASE TWO

THE CONVALESCENCE

I

O rook your pearly gray ruff
Is adorned with kinky follicles
No matter what the foregut regenerates
A posterior may crack at the corners as though it
     were a mouth
Come nearer reader that I may hear you talking to
     yourself
With closed eyes like a cat stealing cream
Om will tell you that transformation is liberation
In whatever form of mask or silence
During cross-talk intensities
Fingernails bitten to the quick are wrestling in the
     dark
Eros concedes that his opponent is Understanding
The guards are bribed the eunuchs drugged
Krishna in the bucket seat of his Lotus knows
The bloodsugar in his brainbank is always overdrawn

II

Phantoms of sand are snaking on through
Whining schoolboys their reluctance overcome
Nose-rings swinging bravely
Are disciplined by the Chief Erection Engineer
He who bears the imprint of a forceps delivery
Respecting no law human or divine
Music from a silver dish
Celebrates the dust-heaps of Calcutta
Baroness Blixen with that lovely hoarse voice of hers
Sang Billie Holiday's I'm a Fool to Want You
The wrinkles didn't matter there was such speed in
     her little body

Antonia! Where's my pocket handkerchief...
At 38th Street and 15th Avenue many people with
        origins in many nations live in a four-storey
        walk-up
What do they *do* — that is the question what they
        think and feel is implied in the answer

III

After being awarded the booby prize for cod banging
His ears went back with a click
Imagining it's cucumber time he struts like a crow
        in the gutter
Eternal mocker upon whom whatever is fourfold
        exists
May the curse of absurdity spermatize his soul
His crutches fall into the K shell
Curd knives undergo rearrangement independent
        of the fluid employed
Angles of rupture and relief
Catapult into caustic soda
Susceptibility is an alligator wrench
Andrade's Creep Law was increased by stretching
In the cream separator the turning is conical
A drop falls from a narrow tube
Urine digests starch

IV

Colonel Buzzard marching his troops down Effluvia
        Lane
Is audible through the lens of the laryngoscope
There's many a bedpan commando

Satisfied with what they have be it only an Arkansas
        toothpick
Or an aerial ladder with nothing to hang upon it
In the still hours of the empty palace I looked in
        every corner
For the cowherd encountered at the turnstile that
        afternoon
He was not hiding anywhere I went to bed clasping
        the cold pillow
And dreamed of a funeral party fit for an outlaw
The nature of this thing is to appropriate anyone
        who comes near
Its aim is to be clinically precise and all but flawless
The reaction is exothermic
A simple inflorescence and you're sitting in the
        resonance clamber of verse structure
Petal is an anagram of plate

V

To alleviate the distress of stocking weavers in
        Nottingham
Flagellar locomotion (principle of the screw)
Fuses with layers of short-toed creations
On the margin of a membrane
In Erosion Close afternoon tea is served by a butler
The celebrants entertained by the bird that flies
        backwards at the sound of abusive language
From the Family Planning Camp on the adjoining
        estate
Mountains in the distance sway like waves in the sea
Or like elations of incoherence
The gamewarden was about to announce an earthquake

Tremors were felt before his labio-dental structure
        could function
The cock's-foot grass bristled and disappeared
Together with many non-tender and compressible
        hearts
Cryptic coloration aiding in the unseen approach
        to make a kill

VI

Conversant with irrationality
The Lake Success sort can be cruel
During periods of alleviation
They've a protective hydrocarbon hard to resist and
        even harder to forget
Ingadeep Sing a believer in All Day Efficiency was
        robbed of his box scraper
Petrolino buried it in the brickyard
When bent around a cylinder, taking first prize in
        the bean-tossing contest
With no permit for impropriety
A clouded sensorium is obtained when bile is mixed
        with sucrose
Foot soldiers who desert the army of the poor
Have a way of correcting the name of the cock-cheese
In Louisiana and Texas sulphur beds are beneath
        400 feet of quicksand
On collapse of the domain the current increases
Bones shed crustacean armor in an opalescent void

VII

Orgasmic declination being sublingual
The vox nihili is something we should understand
Owing to the predominance of feldspar grains
Progress towards puberty was assisted no end
From an oral point of view precocity was pronounced
But I couldn't decide which stage name to choose
Djulfian Scattergram and Bluebeard Fishskull were
      among the rejects
Gumbo Dripstone sounded like the mongrel of
      African Linguistics
Generative semantics won out
Decorated with pseudo-synonyms
English is a stress-timed language with many
      ascending diphthongs
We emerged into a gollactic air bleed
Just in time to hear three shots fired in the park
Where colorless green ideas sleep furiously

VIII

Caracas. Pre-puberty education for the mentally
      defective continued here yesterday
Hedonic bifaciality defined by a Peruvian doctoressa
The genito-anal zone was not slighted
Capillary dilation at mid-gut
Exposed the necessity of gonadectomy in isolated
      cases
Holoparasites are touched upon
And gangliform ecotopes in relation to erectile
      vesiculosa
Gnathopods are graphically expounded
Reminiscent of flame cells of heartwood

Promise of tuberosity is seldom fulfilled
Surreptitiously engaged few hands were raised
Reciprocal enervation brought a welcome change
The critter next to me was going at it
Like a night violet responding with its perfume to
       the nightbird

IX

Is Krishna married no he sleeps on a bone bed
Do you think this will result in increasing
          deformation
Crinkle-marks may be corrected with a brush-
          belt
As long as insertion does not result in tectonics
Alive in the Valley of Elevation
I am not married my brother isn't married my
          sister has been engaged four times
When is your grandparents' wedding anniversary
My grandfather got married in 1921
With no injury to concretionary modules
There were several minor intrusions
Skeletons were dredged from the lake at
          Camp Flyaway
Has the volcanic plug been pulled out for good
The cleavage was a very long time ago
Now we're into the lagoon-phase of the load-cast

X

The destroyer-in-chief's features are distorted by
          a bruise on the cheek
Dressed in full-length anorak with detachable collar

A backward-acting regulator
Re-silvered for gene splicing
Keeps everything at bulb temperature
The afterpulse is monolithic
Excitation depending on the burn-in
Chicanos in brush rockers distribute plastic beads
To the company of free-spending pimps and their
        top prostitutes
But the rum is ruined by Tropicana orangejuice
Heavy metal services and wire-wound resistors
Though subject to human control
Ejaculate on the quartz-crystal slab
Your changeup is good and so is my fastball

XI

Food comes first a sticky banana
For breakfast sheep-hustlers prefer chittlings
What is Djuna holed up in Patchin Place eating at
        this moment
Clandestine the last bite swallowed by
        Harry Crosby
Jean-Arthur had a date in the desert (where else)
There's a fine connection between digestive acids
And alignment for parole
Before the communique his palate was dry as dust
Though poles apart culturally and intellectually
Bernhardt on tour Walt reading to the wounded
Spittle-smeared with glowing tributes
When not playacting both were known to undergo
Altered awareness at the sight of sweetmeats on
        warped mirrors
Bone-marrow stimulation is always elective

XII

Sweat glands are being measured in Seattle
In Cambodia the corrupt elite is put away
Shortselling begins to appear
The Buzzcocks and other punk groups have been
      banned
Taborov's interpolation play had to be recycled
He usually starts with a disposable grid
Or a report from a subdeveloped country
Horns and strings build to repeated peaks
The smoky interface of silence slows down
At a Riviera resort analysts isolate
      the spore clusters of barrel distortion
Vaguely menacing loungers who haunt stretches of
      42nd Street move in among the pack
Fort Napoleon has become a graffiti-scarred
      hangout
Tom Smucker says schlock is materialism in a
      Dionysian mode
Farewell my dearest Evil not every bulbous
      extremity will serve

XIII

The bending moment has arrived
Sun cracks are a factor in its centrosome
A china doll ricochets from the breast drill
The bridal veil of flowering glume
Responds with a fang bolt elongation
Doctor Thapa with more wit than wantonness
Recommends a face hammer for any speech defect
A fungicide spray hits the bridegroom
The wedding guests forget their equations
Amazed by flying foxes from the mangrove swamp

Ramming is followed by finding other words for the
        same thing
Among the secrets leaked was a design for lobate
        incisions
In a three-tiered second class compartment of the
        Delhi-Tinsukia Mail
The newlyweds are in unaccelerated flight

XIV

South of Reaction Rim stands a percussion figure
Loosed from pus pockets packed in wax and sawdust
Double-slip encumbrances yield information
Speech organs play an important part
Calibrated with sheaths of neuromotors
Volumetric glassware disproves statistics
Target trimmings in aluminum foil delighted
        James Joyce
The rhythm was felt as a dummy element
Virgil at the Chelsea: If two He-atoms are placed
        in a box . . .
Stevie Wonder's mastery of the synthesizer
Straightens branches on a dwarf quince
Sacred love lacks angular momentum
The thrust-time characteristic of profane soldiers
Might not the same be said of most prostatic
        cripples

XV

With ruby eyes singed bristles and vestigial wings
The USS Skipjack formerly nuclear-powered
Stripped now of its equipment
No longer nonvanishing at infinity
The very picture of dessication
More useless than the report on the stomach
       contents of 80,000 seagulls
As remote enfin from our concern
As the spiral arms of the Milky Way
Having absorbed as much radiation as soft tissue
       and tendons
With no risk of contamination
The rich-poor gap is plied with kicks to the head
And gold-embroidered padukas
In an arched sewer redolent of the Knot of Brahma
Hit the dog in the water with the force of an
       exotic table lamp

XVI

The presence of germs on the hands of waitresses
Is as common in the Eastern Hemisphere
As basket-case commitments or the endangering of
       wildlife
Antic dispositions add random denouements
Glands traded for declarations of guilt
All the rivulets of middle-age
Alive with eels that flourish in polluted waters
Make it difficult to breathe and speak at the same
       time
Teenage runts steal lunch money from the
       schoolchildren

A Four-H Club orgy is being organized
I muse upon Yukio's auto-erotic immolation
While the joker in the pack lies on a bed of roses
Papa in Montparnasse knew that beer is for
        sustained enjoyment not a shortcut to
        oblivion
No dribble of juice from a plum ran down his chin

XVII

Generously testicled but never a vandal
With a clot which changes shape rapidly
Saint Venant waters the dragon in Cupidon's
        whiskers
A Bulgarian heretic whose unclean linen
Dissolved in cryolite
Comes on with his agony bags
A Muscovite look beginning with the figure 8
Bypassing ultra-violet light to avoid ionization
The Millington Reverberation Formula for
        aromatic compounds
Was internationally accepted in 1954
Diplomats are taken on a familiarizing tour
They'll grab for altitude in Toss-Off Alley
But never alter the extradition treaty
Does your mother want a rabbit

XVIII

One oblique incidence I remember
After the appropriate number of sessions were
        completed

Parasurama and his goon squad arrived
Too late for long-arm inspection
An interplay of cortical exhaustion
Followed biting and scratching as though bad were
        best
Bled dwarfs were in the line-up
They chew on every weed and never get poisoned
If you beat them like spice they smell all the
        sweeter
Leptoids found behind mountains
Feel at home among both new and old stars
No need of seed pathologists or a cleanliness drive
Prior states determine the intensity
Chi semina spine non vada discalge

XIX

The curfew in Bangkok from midnight to 4:30 a.m.
        remains in force
Yeats in his tower Theseus in the labyrinth teach us
        that orbits are only half-integral
Byron in bed
His cock covered with lace bedclothes and syphilis
Must have looked like a noblewoman
Capable of detecting depth of feeling
In a Greek boyfriend so self-sexual he would not
        stop to wonder with whom he should make
        love
But devil tricks devil
The divination ritual is in ribbons
Ambidextrous as a pugilist at a forked road
The disembodied prove the impossible
A minority affairs adviser comes up with an
        utterance

Another shortage of snowtires is expected
Emotional numbness gives way to undisguised
        intoxication

XX

During the incubation period you recovered your
        voice but not your smile
Which once like distant lightning had its moment of
        intensity before vanishing without a trace
The Angel of Desolation obtuse to any inkling that
        the Lilliputian knife-boy who opened her
        carriage door
Was destined to be the bantam weight champion of
        Sussex
Looked at him and thought if you could have your
        say whose severed manhood would you
        choose to have stuffed in your lifeless mouth
Madam my own he might have replied
It never crossed her mind to wonder how he could
        be affected by backdoor spending
And so the conversation with her landscapist
        continued
The proper soil chemistry is maintained if the
        vesicles assume vertical positions
Kindly let me know when the wounded pines are
        up and about
From the spinning master came manual firing and
        a stirring display of shots on the run
Dung Dung pushed the ball out of the goalkeeper's
        reach
And flung his bat away before scampering home
The heat treatment consultant reported a
        dehumanizing appetite for the macabre

XXI

Bless you for that commotion
Trudging in the country like a dean without a
        chapter
Or a cunny-haunted hermit in the days of Queen
        Dick
What double-slung guru dropping wax in the
        desert
Repents of his ways since deflecting from the
        Dirty Shirt Club
Using a phenal rod indicator as a test-tube
He looks upon himself as the Deliverer from
        Significance
And does a perpendicular with the first straggle-
        tail out of the oasis
If he marries which he never will he'll have all his
        buttons on
Dressed like a page in scarlet and sepia
Crowned with hawkmoths
His beard splitter growing symmetrically
Hornic motion is like a flexible string
A sub-image dredged from Ox-Bow Lake

XXII

He who buys flesh buys groans
A Napoleonic carriage rattles through darkened
        streets
Though beauty is potent the biggest calf is not the
        sweetest veal
In drawstring shorts and out-of-date hat
The butcher looked for his knife it was in his mouth
After the sweat of a universal packing
Eating the flickle he refused to be shy

Here's an almond for the parrot who goes mad
        twice a year
Don't break the egg in my apron be still and have
        thy will
Catching fish is not the whole of fishing
Mud chokes no eels
Handsomely as a bear picks muscles
The pig-boy and the punk-pusher play the beast
        with two backs
Before ingesting French vanilla in an unmarked
        van

XXIII

All faces are flowers
Warts add naught to cleft palates
If care is taken with the intraluminosity
Bone scans may solve a few things
You can go back to bed now
Tomorrow I stay home and trim my lover's
        corkscrew toenails
Or else start a sonnet sequence
This vertigo is episodic
Essence of the persona
A topping of Bavarian cream is what I really want
You'll find out how self-rising cornstarch functions
And learn that like a rubber tree you may develop
        maximum yield from minimum stimulation
With no jostling in the queues
And what of the inflammatory corrida

XXIV

(for Harold Stevenson)

Bacteria equipped with non-bacterial functions
Are like roses color of violets
To aid in evacuating U.S. nationals
From a mental security hospital overrun with dogs
El Cordobés, 38, stopped at the door in his white
     Rolls Royce convertible
The bone growth from his head shown clear as a
     fiery pearl
Why is there no yellow fever in India he asked the
     secret service agent doubling as doorman
Then himself gave the answer Because there are too
     many believers in individual terror
Cacti can count and add up to twenty an inmate on
     the second floor yelled down
As who should say in a feeding frenzy
Some undiagnosable malady manipulates our
     contradictions
Listen you son-of-a-bitch the ex-bullfighter shouted
     don't you understand the English Language
Then with his Rhodesian chrome headlights
     flashing off and on
Drove screechingly away from what is said to be the
     most scientific prison anywhere

XXV

After filing a request for a discharge on the basis
     of ill-health
In the airport lounge he wonders if the hand

grenade clutched by his slip-rings will be
    detected
Two assasin-heroes cannot be parallel to a third
Is there anything to hustle in this public room
I don't like taking notes at a trial
The range of coherence lasts no longer than honey
    on a fork
Doctor Brawfort said the more you cry the less
    you'll piss
Even when treated with potassium iodide
Mercurial to the point of speech pathology
The scattering vector lies on the surface
Snake-beings are hungry for lemon-veal birds with
    parsley rice
A handkerchief unfurls as though a food-web of
    sub-mucosa
Were laid lightly on the stomatopodium
No Wildean giftware for biological emotions

XXVI

Have you felt the shrimp in the pocket of his
    campaign coat
There's Beau Cod hawking his brawn
Arms outstretched emitting a cackling sound
For a little something more he'll bury a Quaker
And leave to others the option of joining the crutch
    and toothpick parade
Captain Queernabs of Carrion Row
Wears a weight suspended from pierced nipples
When the skin of the perimeters is anti-parallel
A white ring is formed as though by the
    intervention

Of intelligent beings in a rotating furnace
Every slop master knows
How to make do without another canteen stinker
And to say membrum virile in twelve languages
One for each of the Apostles

XXVII

A pink rat is eating blue butter
Unaware of the poison pitched on the plate its snout
        rises nastily
Billy Turniptop is delighted it was he who prepared
        the bar of Breakstone's best (unsalted)
He watches the rodent expire like a belly ruffian
Aw go to hell and help your sweet niece make a
        pitch-pie he snorts
To the already blubber-headed plague-spreader
How could he know he's done away with a sacred
        animal the companion of Ganesh
Having stymied many a one around the Liverpool
        docks
And once in a nook on the orlop deck
A nibble on his beef-stick woke him
Are you so cock-smitten he cried with all the ardor
        of a bash-bazouk
You don't know when a smith blade will start a
        colonic opening and finish at your vestigial
        cortex
The ships's bells went rotten and rang in reverse
Birds of passage overhead seemed a bit stiff

PHASE THREE

THE RECOVERY

I

(for Morton Gurewitch)

When the self-image is kept at starting point
Our comic ego roams the world
As though the choice of everything included
      nothing
Or anything was there for the asking
In reality from the unrealized future
To the unreal past the present made of neither
Seeking and rejecting partaking of both
The gift of the instant being reserved for the Irish
We'll content ourselves with Indian hemp
Swallow smoke rings for Saint Patrick
In the first row James Hunt of Britain at the wheel
      of his McLaren
Effortless in effort unattached in love
What the fire is burning is not the fire
But take away the substance and the flame goes out

II

The sky-colored prince whom they call Krishna
Unfading urchin symbol of the Way
Bearing February violets color of cows' udders
Said if I am a god it is only because I was born
      of a goddess
Happy is he to whom the sun bares its teeth
The daughter of the demon Madhu overheard
She had just left the sickroom of the walking eagles
Approaching like the British Concorde with ominous
      wings

And bloodless lips of vicious afflictions
Stand up Garuda said Vasudeva's progeny
For marriage functions spacious halls and furnished
        bedrooms
The Oriental Electric and Engineering Company
        is holding auditions
Muslim youth of 22 wanted for an exceptionally
        pretty convent-educated girl of 18
Only the Nubian with flute in hand is living for
        those who love him

III

Decadence is important there is always new matter
        to decay
Chisel-teeth crunch at the transom flap
With no intention of beating the child to death
My usually balanced basket cells failed me
An autonarcosis of the nervous system
Unpredictable as bio-luminescence
The implantation moves to the funnel
In a phase of recuperation whether to bifurcate
Or attend to the hind-gut
Opens into cardiac jelly
The Pasha's courier could not recall
Which tribesman hunting pigs was impaled on his
        own javelin
And fainted dead away after delivering the message
As when lead melts and flows off leaving an
        enriched scum

IV

Astride the chiffonier of the post-oral conductions
The Super-volutes of a key-hole saw
Reveals wounds glistening with aureomycin
The attackers apparently Hispanic youths
Lying on a pile of mismatched lumber
Flank a lefthand screwdriver draped with cloth
     of estate
Johnny Minotaur examines each still-life in turn
Keeping time with his thighs he strips the railroad
     furniture of its slings
All the vasa deferentia are smashed
The sieve of Eratosthenes is in pieces
Tucked in a systalic toga
The virgule of an unknown artist gives him away
Only the vesicula seminalis escape unscathed
Overhead helicopters are searching the rooftops

V

You cannot learn too much about the one you
     idolize
A pattern for all poets
As well as for the criminally insane
The hand of transduction
Belongs to a critical care nurse
More than children are born of loving
Tempering with the balance of nature
White ash on the winds of heaven
Before sending the march into sudden death
     overtime
Rapists with a typhoon in the breast
Exchange beauty for hurt

Never buy anything except a ticket
The verbal is not the least of unemphatic marvels
The body needs sleep like slumber needs love

VI

When a throwback to autogenesis takes place
A wanderer is a frightened man
Ruffian in a flounced costume
Tatters hanging from his bones
Tennysonian fronds and Swinburnian labia
Bailjumper swooning on an asteroid mission
Schooled in the Cult of the Double Axe
Still troubled but normal he's not perfect
Wearing rings at prices unheard of at home
Brass holster rivets provide quality touches
Associated Cut Flowers went out of business
And when do lovers go unburied
All that will be left is an image
Standing in the doorway of sleep

VII

Wanderers in Delirium
Return with unforgettable messages
Concretions of a moment's hesitation
Rebecca! exclaimed Ivanhoe this is not a maiden's
        pastime
Unable to hang itself beneath the floorboards
An elephant in the castle has a fit on the mat
Dyes without antimony entail no afterglow
Ram's book is lost his coat is wet he is ready to do
        anything for the sake of money

Beside the skeleton of a youth aged 20 diggers
        found a five-inch leaden cylinder shaped like
        a phallus
A man whose life I saved after he had been tossed
        by a buffalo attempted to spear the lion
        mangling my servant
I said thank you I am quite well how are you
Poverty is staring him in the face
Could the state run businesses better than the
        people who are now in charge
Some say it could not be done and this is one of the
        things boys and girls have to think about

VIII

The leg of a squashed mosquito on a blinding wall
Throws a very fine shadow
Memphis ran out of flowers
How can they score with only bastinadoes
I do not intend to give you pain but to remind you
        of suffering
Profit-taking in need of extra-terrestrial
        intelligence
Skin-resonance reacting to the destruction of
        language
One of the faintest hints of what it was to be alive
In contrast to sludge in the pontoon
Recreated fragments left by a loner
Attracted to children and bestiality
A dependence on past appeal rather than surprise
Or any hollow in the head of the heart of wherever
Is a poem a forced confession

IX

You see the shadows sharpest
When their unharnessed days
Are no sooner self-abiding than absconding
Nomadic herdsmen of an endless tribe
Wanderings renewed the wanderers constant
Enveloped in psychic sickness or any other aura
Expense of spirit in a waste of shame
The bee whispering in your ear then buzzing off
Not the last but the next to last way to go
Taking it all with you leaving it all behind
As we do every day when it's not the other way
        around
I mean being left nothing nor taking anything
Winner and loser in one's particular precinct
The consequence being inconsequential

X

(Happy Landing for Jonathan Williams)

The secret of shooting is to stay where you are
Isn't this true of any elastic medium
Or of any love life
He takes along his traveling bathroom
Supportive therapy for peak pulse power
Mounted on the expendable liquid tank
Rolling in her neck with his hands when the whip
        slipped
He forgets about range conservation
And the vegetable substitute for a living sacrifice
Rosehips missing in action
Craniopuncture in the combat zone

Preoccupations for our immunologist
Engine tailoff increasing the velocity
As one graphite layer slides over another

XI

Like a pre-genital Bog Trotter
Deformed by thermodynamics
Investigating the products of spin-orbit coupling
Baudelaire sanctified the energies of lunacy
Onto the cause of the swelling of gelatine
He knew why the powder of flowers of sulphur
Floats in bile salts but not in a pint of cochineal
      dye
Working on the enhancement of a spark discharge
He was interrupted by his mulatto mistress who
      burst into the mansard
A gram of gallium of arsenide in the cleft of her
      bosom
She indended to poison his beloved cat and she did
Such an irreversible process could take the clinkers
      out of your bum
Even Charles's drumstick hesitated
Before doing another dive in the dark

XII

She gave what shc could but not always what she
      could have
Horror with elegance is a sure-fire combination
Speaking of frontal lobotomy on an estranged wife
You keep your health and your health keeps you
Like a rioting fish putting up a stiff resistance
A nasal swab to alleviate foetal claustrophobia

Useful remedy while under house arrest
As far from meat and other aphrodisiacs
As Jupiter's twelve heaven-clad moons
Priapism may occur before the age of 2
The vesicles are short-lived
Close to a life-size photo of the downtrodden
But clear as hallucination
Prior to their cannibalizing stolen cars

XIII

Two brothers who escaped from the Rahway
          Minimum Security Camp
Using a deception signal of average brightness
Are intercepted near the acoustics chamber
By an operator in the Central Identification
          Laboratory
In a beam-hole of the bleeder current
These discarnate playmates unaccustomed to
          perfumed garments
Are paralysed by a wordless cry
Programmed as machine-language prosody
The basic access method is a flame to cut a wire
The aging process rendered aeromagnetic
Pushed out of the Nowhere of Asia Minor
Stragglers are pulling the body of a midget through
          marsh grass
Dead space in a glass envelope is handed to the
          controller
Thus promoting spending when times are hard

XIV

Relieved of the family jewels in an agony of tears
All the boon molls of Alakali Canyon
Gather to see them fall like birds from the nest
Of a chanticleer who may never chant again
Call him a clodskull favored by zerophytes
Many a plot for his capture went awry
Until cornered by a roustabout in Connaught
      Circus
Of no avail his prayers to the Eighth Incarnation
Crawling like a baby with one arm raised
Both his charlies a-bounce until they bit the dust
Ineffectual as bumfluff
Or that old cut-plug of Jesse James
Poignancy mined from the cotton belt of burlesque
A wilderness moon rides in the Land of New Ghosts

XV

Stress in the rod's cross-section bores a hole in
      the map
Impeccably rehearsed though vulcanized with
      sulphur
Having learned by heart Shell's law of refraction
In a fit of exhaltation Charles L. flew over the
      Azores
Reconsidering his Last Will & Testament it was not
      to be the last
Though puzzled by the behavior of an erratic river
He was the first infra-sonic hero
Exceptional as a turtle with moveable rib basket
His moon a glass ball in the pocket of a leather
      jacket

No motor retardation no propeller cavitation
The extent of his sensory disturbance
As great as the trajectory New York-Paris
Charged with manic energy
He took his stop sign with him but it wasn't used

XVI

Torture methods of the Guardia are too risky
The state's red light abatement act is not working
Not by will but by imagination
The previous step is never lost
Picabia in his salon Josephine in bananas
Resplendent as spokes of color-breathing
Treasured outbursts of multiple takes
Stylistic integrity brought to blighted
          neighborhoods
Not a single playing card is missing from the
          stacked pack
In nature there's no equality only endless
          adaptation
You've got two other bodies each with a three-fold
          knot
At the Youth Correction and Reception Center what
          is there to miss
Passivity is no solution
Curve your tongue slightly at the end of the second
          syllable

XVII

Military officers are satisfied the situation in the
          country has improved
Arrow worms have broken into the passageways

Bunkers are carted from the streets
Mercenaries guarding important places have been
        recalled
Hair is stroked and signals pass along a sensory
        nerve to the spinal column
Hardened by continence they are sucking amino
        acids
And singing like a gardener bringing water up the
        stairs
Recalling the Deputy Governor's speech in praise
        of prostitution
Not one more member but the member once more
Dingle dangle in need of high-impact insulation
Is it not tired of capering in front of you
Third leg more like a bamboo saw
The length of the root measured in sea squirts
That's the point about tomorrow it's always here

XVIII

Since all is all-important what we are doing is
        not neglecting
Wherever we abide is our native land
Like a cockroach in a maze
The ghetto psycho took this for granted
Gathering voiceprints of songbirds
An experience of endurance in an abnormal
        situation
He thought he would make it until he didn't
And so though not an endangered species
He was placed under preventitive detention
His high cheek-boned face and Roman nose make
        an unpromising start
Cutting leather with a jet of water

But he flies away gracefully the first to escape
And disappears with an owl's sound
Married men smell different

XIX

I would like to have seen Rupert Brooke and King
        Shrigalava making love
The poet's rosy-skinned testes smooth as a twelve-
        year-old's
His Majesty's weapon sheathed like a Hindu
        fisherman's glans held swollen to bursting
        point by a rawhide cockring studded with
        diamonds
Semen clear as saliva slid from the two prostates
Scrotum-colored lips closed with pain-killer finality
        over the Englishman's mouth
Warrior courtiers with peacockfeather fans stood by
Their loincloths fluttered and subsided
They were fascinated by the sheer dimension of
        the ivory lingam
Eyes narrowed to slits as they watched every move
Every motion was interpreted as a homage to Shiva
In the palace there are no air-conditioned rooms
        or color TV
But while cocoanut sherbets melt under your
        tongue
It is nice to be bathed by a slave smelling of musk
Though his foreskin might taste as if water of the
        Arabian Sea had dried upon it

XX

Only spirit can know spirit
Early manhood according to some religions
Is the period in which the animal is killed and the
        head sent under refrigeration to a
        government-designed enclave
At the trailing edge a helical antenna is posted
In the urgency of noontime darkness
The first fruit pulse is wrapped in fishpaper
The forcing function a free-wheel dynatron
Its capillary attraction equivalent to a three-story
        printing press
The advantage of the young is nothing compared to
        the sway of a hairy tongue
Simulating the sounds of unstruck structures
Nice ride says Sinatra emerging from an elevator
To be famous is one thing to be a legend
Is similar but more like the skull shapes of cats
        and humans
Towards which we strive

XXI

Can you conceive of a coastline without need of
        slum clearance
Or of a body that craves no darkness
In a doorless hall I saw the shadow of the shapeless
Absolve me of the cant of the deliberate O Lord
Before joining the merchant marine
Narcissus was sprinkled with jasmine water
Like Tony Agnello at Melville's grave
Blind flying puts him in a tender frenzy
High on universal ether

He would have us attacking Queen Anne's lace by
        remote control
Our Signal Intelligence law enforcement officer
Is just another media fraud
The pigeon in the isolation chamber
Prefers that we act like normal people leading
        customary lives

XXII

Dangers of the swimmingpool are incomparable
In the Sicilian Defence white obtains a spatial
        advantage
Water for cloud walkers is negative and magnetic
And should be avoided like Milton's daughters or
        an ex-president's grammar
Events come to people some are painted with
        cocaine
Nymphokicks of configural conditioning
Hadrian competing with saturation tremors
Deemed it easier to live an original life than to die
        an original death
A flanking feint in a bid for isolation
Praised for his crab-bat as the horniest of old
        soldiers
He had that last ride below the crupper
In the Cairo museum Rameses harbors fungi and
        insects
Should a poet be sentimental about poetry
Lizard behind the curtain are you looking for
        stolen rain

XXIII

Dressed in a dhoti with scarf of yellow silk
Involatile as a charioteer on a visit to Uddhava's
    stud farm
The image is waiting for a hand to be laid on its
    forehead
Just as we must wait for the sun to burn away the
    mist
And to be told you are beautiful
Knowing that what stands revealed may be either
    real or unreal
So long as we know not what it is but what it means
Whether gold in the morning silver at noon or
    lead at night
All that is sharp is short
Happy the corpse the rain rains on
Tennyson a lad of fourteen wrote on a rock
    Byron is dead
The time of de-lousing is a cancelled occasion
The King murdered in his castle was buried
    privately his eyes like piss-holes in the snow
On the grave sits a young frog undisturbed by the
    cold winter wind

XXIV

My precision of feeling is your lack of
    comprehensibility
A poetry of post-poetry to be published
    posthumously
Meaningless to try to be convinced of yourself
Believe like John Donne only in something outside
Whether or not you had anything to do with it

Whatever is extraneous like the hoop trapped by
        ching-Kuang-fa in the first half of the last
        inning
He toed it home as though guiding the wisdom of
        accident
A self-made man to be understood as automatic
Safeguarding the interests of illiterates
Pressing for the expression of history
Differentiating them from oil-driven intensifiers
The book of repetition which we have no time to
        read
Everyone's unfinished magnum opus
Dedicated to the white-watered one who knows all

XXV

Enacting the role of the marvelous traveler
Krishna is like a hospital said Ali he accepts all
        germs
Part of that ridge near the dorsal surface is
        heteromorphous
Not in its harmonies but as one less reassurance
The implementation being uncharacteristic
Like the voluptuousness of buying things one can
        do without
Your conduct is unaccountable
In a medieval city put to the torch by Germans
The birds are back birds with dry feathers and
        warning songs
A landing site picture of total separateness
The quanta of the fields
Epitomizing the great flow and magic name of
        Indra
Oh not to move not even with the mind
Until the masterpiece has been mastered

XXVI

Indra with his string of pearls
Sometimes pulls the destruct switch
The mornings go past
Without a prayer to your fetish
No offense should be given to the deity of rain
In one of the ten beds of the Youth Hostel at Puri
Sleeps a Nipponese traveler painted by Pavlik
Jockey Hari Singh has a hot center
Disappearing into Sri Lanka for a month I was
          quite visible to the Ceylonese
Placing a small coin in the cowdung which covered
          the hand of a little girl whose photo I took as
          she stood in the dooryard guarded by two
          elephants of blue clay
The Synthesis is what I made and what has made
          me
But love lasts longer than fame for many another
Whatever the waves are saying will be cradled by
          the wind
Leaving skull-silver mirrors to keep you wondering

XXVII

What seems like fragmentation is making all in one
Tchelitchew Excelsior of sensory disturbances
Prophet turning round and round an opening
Avian respiration in everything he did
Tidal in certain regions a medium in which to
          propagate
Each scan of ancestry
Excess of subtlety from the enchanter's hand
Grounded planets in process of formation

Particles of zero rest-mass
Linger on the lips of the life-class
Visceral arches of aboriginal waveforms
He left them as he found them unconverted
Ginseng roots wrenched from their circuits
Mix with the dregs of a dreamless sleep

Set in 12 point Baskerville and printed on Warren's Olde Style on
the Heidelberg Kord at the Open Studio Print Shop, Rhinebeck, N.Y.,
this first edition consists of 1,000 copies. Of these, twenty-six
copies, lettered A-Z, are signed by the author and handbound by
Alan Brilliant of Unicorn Press, each with a unique collage-print
handcolored and signed by Indra.